THE
PROPHETIC
ADVANTAGE

STUDY GUIDE

THE
PROPHETIC
ADVANTAGE

Michelle McClain

CHARISMA
HOUSE

Most CHARISMA HOUSE BOOK GROUP products are available at special quantity discounts for bulk purchase for sales promotions, premiums, fund-raising, and educational needs. For details, write Charisma House Book Group, 600 Rinehart Road, Lake Mary, Florida 32746, or telephone (407) 333-0600.

THE PROPHETIC ADVANTAGE STUDY GUIDE
  by Michelle McClain-Walters
Published by Charisma House
Charisma Media/Charisma House Book Group
600 Rinehart Road
Lake Mary, Florida 32746
www.charismahouse.com

Cover design by Justin Evans

Instructional Designer: Regine Jean-Baptiste/!Impact Course
Developers

Visit the author's website at
www.michellemcclainwalters.com.

Library of Congress Control Number: 2017935664
International Standard Book Number: 978-1-62999-178-8
E-book ISBN: 978-1-62999-450-5

17 18 19 20 21 — 9 8 7 6 5 4 3 2 1
Printed in the United States of America

As arrows are in the hand of a mighty man;
so are children of the youth. Happy is
the man that hath his quiver full of them:
they shall not be ashamed, but they shall
speak with the enemies in the gate.

—Psalm 127:4–5, KJV

To Eboni, my beautiful, bold apostolic
missionary: Your passion for Jesus and
desire to follow His prophetic purpose
for your life at all costs are inspiring and
challenging. Being your mother is the greatest
joy of my life. I love you so much. Keep
breaking limitations and equipping your
generation with the prophetic advantage.

To all of my spiritual sons and daughters: It is
has been an honor and a privilege to mentor,
train, and equip you to fulfill the God-given
destiny over your lives. I am humbled that
the Lord would allow me to influence so
many of His greatest leaders of tomorrow.
Knowing each one of you has made my life
richer. You will be a part of the generation
that will turn the world upside down.

STUDY GUIDE

INTRODUCTION

THE ABILITY TO hear the voice of God is essential to our human existence. It is perhaps one of the greatest advantages God has given to human beings. When we clearly recognize God's voice, we are afforded an invaluable resource. Hearing God's voice allows us to walk in the promises and blessing for our lives and the lives of those around us. The inability to hear God's voice often leaves us frustrated, overwhelmed, anxious, worried, and sometimes feeling lost and alone. This was never God's intention for you. God's purpose has always been for you to prosper confidently under the leading and guiding of His voice. In addition, the Lord not only wants us to hear God's voice for ourselves but also to hear God for others so that we can become heralds of God's truth, prophetic mouthpieces that transform the lives of everyone we meet.

The book *The Prophetic Advantage*, beginner's video teachings, and this study guide were created to help you embark on the journey of becoming a mouthpiece for God who transforms the world. This study guide and the companion videos are intended to help you discover your prophetic advantage and:

- identify the benefits and blessings of prophecy

- review the different ways God communicates with individuals

- develop your ability to hear the voice of the Lord

- distinguish the character traits that you need to be an effective mouthpiece for God

- create blueprints for transforming the world according to God's prophetic pattern for the local church

The workbook and videos are also filled with the foundational concepts and practical steps you will need to be activated in hearing the voice of God for yourself and others. To that end, each lesson contains similar elements to assist you in clearly understanding and applying the concepts and steps for living in your God-ordained prophetic advantage. Each lesson includes the following sections:

Read

You'll start off by reading an introduction to the key concepts of the lesson. This section will also provide a great review of assigned chapters in the *Prophetic Advantage* book that correspond with the lesson.

Personal Discovery

This section is designed for you to reflect on how to apply the key concept to your life. This is a time to look deeper and consider how the concept translates to your everyday living.

Reflect

You will have the opportunity to prayerfully consider places where God is leading and challenging you to look deeper and learn about yourself and others.

Watch

Gain deeper revelation and inspiration on the lesson through the video teachings.

Group Discussion

Learning is fun when we share and grow with others. This section provides questions and prophetic activations, where you can reflect and practice using the lesson's teachings. Here are some helpful tips:

- If you are using this as an individual study, consider partnering with a spouse, parent, sibling, or friend to reflect and practice hearing the voice of God. When you find a partner, be sure to share the insights, observations, and tips you have learned from the lesson. Encourage that person to join you for personal study as well!

- If you are using this as a small group study, your small group leader will pair you with members of your small group so you can grow and share together.

Action Plan

This section is designed to help you develop a tactical plan to live out the concepts you learned during the lesson.

Notes

This is where you can record your thoughts on the live video teachings. You can also use this part of your lesson to record other insights and observations from your study time.

A leader's guide is available for free download at www .michellemcclainbooks.com to assist in facilitating a group study. The guide includes lesson plans and various templates that can be used to coordinate a small group as well as tips and notes for responding to the lesson questions.

YOU HAVE AN ADVANTAGE!

What advantage then hath the Jew? Or what profit is there of circumcision? Much every way: chiefly, because that unto them were committed the oracles to God.

—ROMANS 3:1–2, KJV

WELCOME TO LESSON one of *The Prophetic Advantage Study Guide*. This lesson is intended to intoduce you to the greatest advantage you have in life. If you have not had a chance to do so, please review the introduction, chapter 1, and chapter 2 of *The Prophetic Advantage* book.

Read

God is calling you. He is inviting you to take hold of an advantage that has been prepared for you since He set the foundation of the world. This advantage is the ability to hear the voice of God. We have an invitation to hear the voice of God not only for ourselves but also for others as we prophesy.

- *Prophecy* is

_____

_____

_____

_____

- To *prophesy* is

_____

_____

_____

_____

_____

- To be *prophetic* is

_____

_____

_____

_____

_____

Why do you believe God gave us the ability to prophesy?

_____

_____

_____

_____

When we align ourselves to hear the voice of God through a relationship with Christ, we gain a prophetic advantage. God gives us this ability because it was never the will of the Lord for us to go through life restless, frustrated, and trying to figure everything out on our own. The prophetic advantage was meant to benefit us in every circumstance and situation we face in life. The ability to hear God's voice enables us to experience the blessings God has assigned for our lives.

Our prophetic advantage also empowers us to bless others through forth-telling and foretelling.

Define *forth-telling prophecy*.

_____

_____

_____

_____

_____

Define *foretelling prophecy*.

_____

_____

_____

_____

_____

The gift of being able to communicate the mind of God and announce His future agenda is not a new phenomenon. We have multiple examples in the Bible of men and women just like you and me who by listening to the voice of God were able to save lives, birth nations, and transform the world. Let's spend some time reviewing some examples in Scripture of various individuals who had an advantage because they could hear the voice of God.

Read Ezra 6:14.

What advantage did God grant because these individuals could hear the voice of God?

_____

_____

_____

_____

_____

What do you imagine would have happened if they had not known this information?

_____

_____

_____

_____

_____

Was this a forth-telling or a foretelling advantage?

_____

_____

_____

_____

_____

Read Judges 4.

How did God help the people?

_____

_____

_____

_____

_____

What was the outcome?

_____

_____

_____

_____

Read 2 Kings 7:1–16.

What benefit did the people experience because there was a prophet who could communicate the mind of God?

_____

_____

_____

_____

Personal Discovery

God has a long history of communicating with His people. Scripture is filled with those stories and serves to remind us that God is still speaking today! The ability to hear the voice of God is our inheritance. This is the prophetic advantage that God has granted you. Our advantage is the capacity to speak to God through prayer and to actually hear, see, and perceive God's communication to us.

When we embrace the truth that we can communicate with God as we would a friend, we reap the benefits of the legacy of prophecy found in Scripture.

Read Psalm 95.

What is God's admonishment for us regarding listening for His voice?

_____

_____

_____

_____

_____

_____

_____

_____

What happens to those who do not listen to the voice of the Lord?

_____

_____

_____

_____

_____

The Bible is filled with promises for those who listen to the voice of God. *The Prophetic Advantage* book outlines several benefits of prophecy, including the following:

- Helps us to prosper

- Encourages us to move into the will of God

- Awakens us to a realm where we can know the purpose and plans for our lives

- Releases faith to operate beyond what we are accustomed to

- Breaks through demonic strongholds

- Restores the dignity and honor human beings lost in the Garden of Eden

Take a moment and think about how you have experienced God's communication to you through forth-telling or foretelling prophecy. Document a time when you had a personal advantage because you heard

God's voice speaking to you. What benefit did you
receive from having this type of advantage?

_____

_____

_____

_____

_____

_____

_____

Reflect

When we encounter the true and living God for ourselves, we gain a new level of responsibility and conviction. We are held accountable for the revelation of God
given to us, and we have the capability to hear and see
humanity from God's perspective. This advantage helps
us to grow into the image and likeness of Christ. We gain
the impartation of Jesus's lionlike character, including
the following:

- Strength

- Valiance

- Fearlessness

- Boldness

Define each of these attributes of the lionlike character of Christ.

- Strength

_____

_____

- Valiance

_____

_____

- Fearlessness

_____

_____

- Boldness

_____

_____

Pick the attribute that you believe is your strength. Which of these attributes do you believe God is calling you to strengthen?

_____

_____

_____

_____

_____

The lionlike character of Christ is a mandate for all who hear the voice of God. Prophetic people must embrace the call to roar in proclamations, decrees, praise, worship, and intercession. When we encounter God's voice for ourselves, our families, our cities, and our nations, yet refuse to move in boldness, we must uncover and counter the hindrance.

What is the biggest hindrance you experience to walking in the strength, valiance, fearlessness, and boldness of Christ's Spirit within you?

Fear is a major factor that keeps us from moving in our God-given prophetic advantage. The enemy seeks to keep us afraid of failure or scared of our own success. Fear can manifest in our lives in different ways.

Consider your biggest fears. How do they hinder you from moving in lionlike boldness?

_____

_____

_____

_____

_____

When God's truth is communicated to us in a prophetic moment, it helps us to become even more like Jesus.

Watch

Let's hear more about the prophetic advantage God has given us. Watch the video teaching titled "You Have an Advantage!"

Group Discussion

The video teaching reminds us that we have the ability to prophesy through the Holy Spirit.

What is the role of the Holy Spirit in prophecy?

_____

_____

_____

_____

_____

Partner with someone in your group to define the sevenfold Spirit of God. Read Isaiah 11:1–4 for a list of the sevenfold Spirit of God.

Define the various expressions of the sevenfold Spirit of God.

1. Spirit of the Lord:

_____

_____

_____

_____

_____

2. Spirit of wisdom:

_____

_____

_____

_____

_____

3. Spirit of understanding:

_____

_____

_____

_____

_____

_____

4. Spirit of counsel:

_____

_____

_____

_____

_____

_____

5. Spirit of might:

_____

_____

_____

_____

_____

_____

6. Spirit of knowledge:

_____

_____

_____

_____

_____

7. Spirit of the fear of the Lord:

_____

_____

_____

_____

_____

Which of the seven attributes of the Spirit of God do you believe is your partner's strongest gift? Which one do you believe God desires to strengthen? Try not to guess; pray and ask God to speak to you concerning your partner's strengths and opportunities for improvement.

_____

_____

_____

_____

The Holy Spirit makes prophecy possible by giving us access to the revelatory realm of God. When we hear the voice of God for ourselves and for others, we can release our Christlike roar against injustice, idolatry, sin, rebellion, and the enemies of God. We are empowered to shine a light for Christ and to point others to righteousness.

Action Plan

God's sevenfold Spirit is expressed within us prophetic people as we roar against injustice, sin and rebellion, idolatry, and the enemies of God.

In the space provided, write the area(s) in which God is calling you to roar. Also list the attributes you need to strengthen that were revealed throughout this lesson by your answers and the responses from your group partner. Spend time in prayer and ask God to release strategies to help you overcome your hindrances to walking in the likeness of Christ. Ask God to communicate to you one quality that you can begin to strengthen as you yield further to the sevenfold Spirit of God.

_____

_____

_____

_____

_____

_____

_____

Notes

_____

_____

_____

_____

_____

_____

_____

_____

_____

_____

_____

_____

_____

_____

_____

_____

_____

_____

Notes

CULTIVATE YOUR CAPACITY TO HEAR THE VOICE OF THE LORD

For God speaketh once, yea twice,
yet man perceiveth it not.

—JOB 33:14, KJV

THIS LESSON IS designed to help you nurture your capacity to hear the voice of God. You will review the different ways God communicates with individuals and develop your ability to hear the voice of God.

Review chapters 7–9 of *The Prophetic Advantage*.

Read

The world is crying out for solutions, guidance, and transformation. We need cures for diseases, leaders with the heart of Christ, and solutions to the social injustices that plague our world. The sevenfold Spirit of God reminds us that the hope of generations past, present, and future is found in the voice of God.

Read Psalm 29.

What are some of the qualities this psalm lists concerning the voice of the Lord?

_____

_____

_____

_____

Which quality of God's voice resonates with you the most? Why?

_____

_____

_____

_____

God's voice has the power to utterly destroy our enemies, consume our hearts with Christ's love, impact and rearrange our lives, and activate and birth new things in our lives in addition to propelling us to action. Therefore, the ability to hear God's voice is an invaluable resource that we must cultivate to transform our world.

Personal Discovery

The Bible recorded multiple accounts when God's voice through forth-telling and foretelling prophecies transformed individuals and met the needs of the world. In order to activate your God-given prophetic advantage, it is important that you understand the ways in which God communicates with you.

Complete the following assessment to help you learn the primary way in which God communicates with you. Read the following statements. Please rank each of the statements in order of most frequent occurrence with one being the most frequent occurrence and twenty being the least frequent occurrence. No number should be used twice. This is not a pass or fail test. This is an assessment to help you identify the primary ways in which God communicates with you. Please rank the statements based on the way you are (as opposed to the way you think you should be). When you are finished, review the assessment results.

_____ A. I often receive special messages about myself or something I was praying about through light, fleeting, and spontaneous thoughts such as an urge or a prompt to take action.

_____ B. I often receive special messages about myself or something I was praying about through a simple picture coming to mind or fleeting imprints of pictures upon my imagination.

_____ C. I often receive special messages about myself or something I was praying about through dreams at night.

_____ D. I often receive special messages about myself or something I was praying about through unplanned and/or intentional meetings, but it is not until I'm in the middle of the meeting or it's over that I recognize its significance.

_____ E. I often receive special messages about myself or something I was praying about when others are speaking.

_____ F. I often receive special messages about myself or something I was praying about in the ordinary, personal moments of my day.

_____ G. I often receive special messages about myself or something I was praying about through a thought.

_____ H. I often receive special messages about myself or something I was praying about through sermons.

_____ I. I often receive special messages about myself or something I was praying about through visions during which I am aware of my physical surroundings yet the vision appears real to my senses.

_____ J. I often receive special messages about myself or something I was praying about when others share a message from God to me through prophecy.

_____ K. I often receive special messages about myself or something I was praying about through nature.

_____ L. I often receive special messages about myself or something I was praying about when I read or watch the news.

_____ M. I often receive special messages about myself or something I was praying about by seeing people healed and God move through miracles.

_____ N. I often receive special messages about myself or something I was praying about through the various situations I face in life.

_____ O. I often receive special messages about myself or something I was praying about when I watch television shows and movies.

_____ P. I often receive special messages about myself or something I was praying about through quiet moments when I can be still and listen for answers to my prayers and concerns.

_____ Q. I often receive special messages about myself or something I was praying about through dance or live action dramas set to music.

_____ R. I often receive special messages about myself or something I was praying about through wind, snow, rain, cold, and heat weather patterns.

_____ S. I often receive special messages about myself or something I was praying about through dreams that encourage my faith.

_____ T. I often receive special messages about myself or something I was praying about by trusting my feelings and ideas.

Circle the letter in the list below that corresponds to the statement you rated as your number one most frequent occurrence. Record your answer. This is your primary way of hearing the voice of God. Then, circle the statements you ranked two through five in the list to identify other ways God has communicated with you.

A. Impressions

B. Visions

C. Dreams

D. Circumstances

E. Preached messages

F. Circumstances

G. Impressions

H. Preached messages

I. Trances

J. Divine decree

K. Weather

L. Newspapers

M. Signs and wonders

N. Circumstances

O.   Television

P.   Still small voice

Q.   Prophetic drama

R.   Weather

S.   Dreams

T.   Impressions

My primary way of hearing the voice of God is

_____

I also hear God's voice through:

1. _____

2. _____

3. _____

4. _____

Do you agree with the assessment that this is your primary way of hearing God's voice? Why or why not?

_____

_____

_____

_____

_____

_____

Did some of the other statements resonate with you as well? Why do you think you partially related to some of the other statements?

_____

_____

_____

_____

_____

How can you continue to cultivate and strengthen your primary method of hearing the voice of God?

_____

_____

_____

_____

_____

There are the many ways God communicates with us. Take a moment to provide definitions for these methods of communication. Use pages 113–118 in the *Prophetic Advantage* book for help defining these methods of hearing God's voice. God communicates to us through the following:

- Impressions

_____

_____

_____

_____

- Still small voice

_____

_____

_____

_____

- Visions

_____

_____

_____

_____

- Dreams

_____

_____

_____

_____

Lesson 2

- Television

_____

_____

_____

_____

- Newspapers (world events)

_____

_____

_____

_____

- Trances

_____

_____

_____

_____

- Circumstances

_____

_____

_____

_____

- Preached messages

_____

_____

_____

_____

- Divine decree

_____

_____

_____

_____

- Prophetic drama

_____

_____

_____

_____

- Weather

_____

_____

_____

_____

- Signs and wonders

_____

_____

_____

_____

Review the list of ways in which God communicates with us. Place a check next to any of the communication methods listed that you did not previously know God could use to communicate to people. Now that you are aware of these communication methods, you can become more intentional and open to receiving God's communication through these methods.

Go back through the list and document any experience you have had in the past with any of the communication methods.

_____

_____

_____

_____

_____

_____

_____

_____

Reflect

The voice of the Lord is connected to the presence of the Lord. Whenever we encounter the presence of God, we can expect to hear the voice of God. We can be assured that God desires to speak to us as much as we desire to hear His voice. Scripture reminds us in Psalm 95:7 that we are the Lord's sheep, and we hear His voice. He leads us and guides us by His voice. Therefore, we can cultivate the voice of the Lord as we grow in relationship with our Great Shepherd. An authentic relationship with the Lord brings us into God's presence and allows us to hear His voice of comfort and guidance.

We can also cultivate our ability to hear the voice of God through the following:

- Worship

- Knowledge of God's Word

- Building relationship with God through prayer and intercession

- Fasting

- Prophecy

Which of these methods do you currently use to grow in your ability to hear the voice of the Lord?

_____

_____

Why do you use this particular method?

_____

_____

_____

_____

What is something you can do to be more consistent in cultivating the voice of God?

_____

_____

_____

_____

If you currently are not practicing any of these methods, identify one method and something you can do to strengthen your ability to hear the voice of the Lord.

_____

_____

_____

_____

Watch

Check out the video teaching titled "Cultivate the Voice of the Lord" to learn more tips on how you can grow in hearing the voice of the Lord.

Group Discussion

As we cultivate our ability to hear the voice of the Lord for ourselves, we can also grow in the ability to hear the voice of the Lord for others. God's desires to not only speak to us but also to speak through us concerning the lives, situations, and destinies of others. The Lord wants to use us to prophesy to others in a way that transforms their lives and points them to the goodness of God.

Grab a partner and begin cultivating your ability to hear the voice of the Lord by listening and sharing with that person what God desires to communicate to him or her. Use the following activations to help you share God's voice with your partner.

After you both have shared what God has communicated to you, find another partner within the group and share with that person what God is leading and guiding you to say using some of the activations listed below.

Select one of the activations below. Take a moment to pray and ask God what to communicate to your partner concerning the topic. For example, if you selected the first topic, you would pray and ask, "God, what color does [insert partner's name] represent to You?" When you hear an answer, you would pray again and ask God, "Why? What does that mean?" Then you would share what the Lord communicated to you. Now, choose one of the topics below and begin listening for God's voice.

- What color does this person represent to God? You represent the color _____ to God because _____.

- What season does this person represent to God? You represent the _____ season because _____.

- What room does this person represent to God? You represent the _____ room because _____.

- What movie character does this person represent to God? You represent the movie character _____ because _____.

- What comic book character does this person represent to God? You represent the comic book character _____ because _____.

- What Bible character does this person represent to God? You represent the Bible character _____ because _____.

- What book of the Bible does this person represent to God? You represent the Book of

_____ in the Bible because

_____ .

- What form of water does this person represent to God? You represent the _____ form of water because

_____ .

- Ask God for a Bible verse for your partner. Why does God want to communicate this verse to your partner?

- Ask God for a word that describes your partner. Why did God want to communicate this word to your partner?

- What is one area in which God desires to minister to your partner? Why does God want to communicate to this aspect of his or her life?

- Ask God for a message to communicate to your partner concerning one area of his or her life.

- Ask God for a picture of something He desires to communicate to your partner.

- Ask God to let you know the emotion He feels concerning your partner.

- Ask God for areas He would like you to pray for concerning your partner. Why does

God want you to pray for this particular area? What does He desire to communicate to your partner about this area?

- Ask God for an encouraging word to share with your partner. Why does God want to share that word with your partner?

- Ask God for a specific phrase that will resonate with your partner. Why does God want to communicate that phrase?

- Ask God for a meaningful street name for your partner. What does God want to communicate to your partner through this meaningful street name?

- Ask God for a meaningful number for your partner. What does God want to communicate to your partner through this meaningful number?

- Ask God for a single meaningful word for your partner. What does God want to communicate to your partner through this one meaningful word?

- Ask God for a meaningful sentence for your partner. What does God want to communicate to your partner through this meaningful sentence?

Lesson 2

- Ask God for a meaningful song for your partner. What does God want to communicate to your partner through this meaningful song?

- Ask God to communicate some things about your partner's past. Why does God want to share this particular point about your partner's past?

- Ask God to communicate some things about your partner's present. Why does God want to share this particular point about your partner's present?

- Ask God to communicate some things about your partner's future. Why does God want to share this particular point about your partner's future?

Tips for Sharing a Prophetic Word

Here are some tips for sharing a prophetic word with your partner during this exercise:

- Only speak what the Lord has given you.
- Your word should bring edification, exhortation, and comfort. If you believe you are receiving a word of warning or a directive word for someone, pray. Then submit it to someone else you know who can clearly hear the voice of the Lord. Ask that person to help you judge what you are hearing and to help you pray for your partner.
- Use your normal speaking voice, look your partner in the eye, and act normally when sharing the voice of God. Always avoid mysticism.
- Take special care not to be negative, condescending, or belittling to your partner.
- God allows us to make our own choices and decisions; refrain from being directive.
- Don't give words of rebuke or bring correction.
- Refrain from giving harsh warnings.
- Don't prophesy marriages, pregnancies, future dates, or the sex of babies.
- Allow your partner to apply, fill in the blanks, and disagree with the prophetic word.
- If you miss it, apologize, and don't get discouraged.
- *Always* thank God for speaking His word and thank the person.

Use the following table to keep track of the prophetic words you receive from your partner(s). You can also use it for notations. If you hear something that you do not feel you should share or that does not align with the tips provided, write it down in the notes section. Then talk with the facilitator about what you heard. Allow the leader to determine whether what is written should be shared.

Date	Prophetic Word	Notes

Action Plan

It is important to note that just because we can hear the voice of God, it does not mean we are prophets. Serving in the office of a prophet is very serious business. When we begin to hear the voice of God, it is an invitation to draw closer to God's presence through the power of the Holy Spirit. There is great diversity in the prophetic realm; there is the spirit of prophecy, the gift of prophecy, and the office of a prophet.

The office of the prophet involves calling, training, and commissioning. Prophets receive a special calling from God into the office. Even after God calls a prophet, this does not automatically put them in the office of a prophet. There must be a significant amount of training. Prophets must be trained in the ability to hear the voice of God and other aspects of the office of the prophet. Even being called and trained does not make an individual a prophet. There also must be a commissioning to step into the office.

Practice, practice, practice is important to hearing the voice of God! Select one of the verses below. Read the verse and ask God to show you a picture vision or give you a sentence that will be relevant to you concerning this scripture. Journal the revelation God gives you by writing down what you saw or heard. Feel free to draw pictures when possible. How does the message God gave resonate with you?

Psalm 103:20–22 (NKJV):

Bless the LORD, you His angels, who excel in strength, who do His word, heeding the voice of His word. Bless the LORD, all you His hosts, you ministers of His, who do His pleasure. Bless the LORD, all His works, in all places of His dominion.

Psalm 26:7–8 (NKJV):

That I may proclaim with the voice of thanksgiving, and tell of all Your wondrous works. LORD, I have loved the habitation of Your house, and the place where Your glory dwells.

Jeremiah 50:2 (NKJV):

Declare among the nations, proclaim, and set up a standard; proclaim—do not conceal it.

_____

_____

_____

_____

_____

_____

Isaiah 61:1–2:

To proclaim liberty to the captives, and the opening of the prison to those who are bound; to proclaim the acceptable year of the LORD.

_____

_____

_____

_____

_____

_____

Notes

Notes

_____

_____

_____

_____

_____

_____

_____

_____

_____

_____

_____

_____

_____

_____

_____

_____

_____

_____

_____

ASCEND THE HILL OF THE LORD

Blessed are the pure in heart,
for they shall see God.

—MATTHEW 5:8

THE ABILITY TO hear the voice of God is the beginning of the journey that prophetic people must take to ascend the hill of the Lord and move into a deeper relationship with Christ. This lesson is designed to help you go deeper in your relationship with the Lord as you distinguish the character traits you need to be an effective mouthpiece for God. Review chapter 5 of *The Prophetic Advantage* book.

Read

As our hearts are intentionally opened to hear the voice of the Lord, God invites us to go into a deeper relationship with Christ. The more you are willing to hear the voice of God for yourself, the easier it is to become a prophetic person who can hear the voice of God for others. It is on this journey that God extends to us a question that can take us into deeper realms of His presence. On the road to growing and prospering from our ability to hear God's voice, the Lord asks us according to Psalm 24:3, "Who may ascend the hill of the LORD? Who may stand in His holy place?"

In Scripture, hills and mountains are secret meeting places with the Lord. So, to ascend the hill of the Lord is to start the process of relinquishing your nature for that of Jesus Christ. When we accept the offer to embrace a deeper relationship with Christ, it opens the possibility for God to change our nature by:

- making us look like Jesus and birthing the character of Christ within us

- challenging our inadequacies

- challenging our fears

- recalibrating how we see ourselves and how we see others

- permitting God to make us into what He wants us to be

How do you think God begins to accomplish these tasks of changing our nature?

_____

_____

_____

_____

_____

How can we experience a changed nature? What is our responsibility?

_____

_____

_____

_____

God realizes the task of transforming our nature by leading and guiding us by His voice. He will speak to us about changes we must make in our personality and character, help us to surrender, and assure us when we are on the right track to becoming like Christ. It is our duty to keep a willing heart and to always come back to the hill to ascend higher in the presence of the Lord.

What does a deeper relationship with God look like for you in this season of your life?

_____

_____

_____

_____

_____

Ask God to reveal to you the areas of your nature He desires to change. Be sure to ask God why He desires to change those particular areas at this time.

_____

_____

_____

_____

_____

Be sure to document your experience as you embrace God's desire to see your nature changed into the likeness of Jesus Christ.

Personal Discovery

When God begins to change our nature, it is to build the characteristics of Christ within us that we need to be an effective mouthpiece for God. The greatest weapon prophetic people have is their hearts, because according to Luke 6:45, out of the abundance of the heart the mouth speaks. This means that whatever is in your heart will most likely overflow onto others and upon yourself. This is because the heart is the lens by which we relay the voice of the Lord to others and seek to understand God's voice for ourselves.

Therefore, as a prophetic people, we must consistently work on our hearts by developing and desiring that God birth the characteristics of Christ within us. Jesus, the Chief Prophet, also serves as the chief example for those who are prophetic. He possessed all the characteristics that make someone an effective communicator of God's heart and mind. Jesus's words continue to be powerful well over two thousand years after He lived upon the earth because they aligned with His character. The following qualities characterized Jesus's ability to be God's mouthpiece:

- Walk of love

- Humility

- Purity

- Holy conversation

- Servanthood

In your own words provide a definition for each of these Christlike characteristics. Use Scripture to inform your definitions.

- Walk of love

_____

_____

_____

_____

- Humility

_____

_____

_____

_____

- Purity

_____

_____

_____

_____

- Holy conversation

_____

_____

_____

_____

- Servanthood

_____

_____

_____

_____

Now that you have a deeper understanding of the Christlike character that God desires to birth within you, take a moment to conduct some self-reflection and identify what is in your heart.

Consider how well you exemplify the characteristics of Christ. Rate yourself according to the godly characteristics of an effective mouthpiece of God on a scale from one to five, with one being excellent and five representing the need for significant improvement.

_____ Walk of love

_____ Humility

_____ Purity

_____ Holy conversation

_____ Servanthood

Select the lowest score listed among the Christlike characteristics. Pray and ask God for a scripture you can study relating to this topic. Write a prayer below asking God to build godly characteristics within your

heart. Include in your prayer your commitment to become an effective mouthpiece for God.

_____

_____

_____

_____

_____

_____

_____

Continue to study and meditate on the scripture God gave you concerning the area of your heart in which there is a need for significant improvement.

Reflect

The more we ascend the hill of the Lord into a deeper relationship with God, the more our nature and character changes into that of Jesus Christ. Jesus was known for His ability to see life and others from God's perspective. He mastered meekness, pursued holiness, and served others well. In John 12:49, Jesus reminds us that His conversations were holy when He says, "For I have not spoken on My own authority, but the Father who sent Me gave Me a command, what I should say and what I should speak." Jesus's commitment to say only what God said and do only what God did allowed Him to always keep holy conversations.

Yet perhaps Jesus's most notable character trait is His

deep love for others. The source of Jesus's capacity to heal, deliver, minister, and even go to die on the cross for us is rooted in the love of God. Being rooted in the love of God enabled Christ to be a pure vessel who could communicate the voice of God in the lives of others, and doing so transformed the world.

In the same way, those who have accepted the call to be God's mouthpiece and transform the world must develop their love for both God and others. The love of God must become our pursuit. We are to seek God with our whole heart. Jeremiah 29:13 promises that if we seek God wholeheartedly, we will find Him. God will respond to our desire to walk even deeper in His love. The more we are filled with the love of God, the easier it becomes to love others. When the love of God is the source by which we communicate God's heart to others, we will begin to see the transformation in our world.

Walking in the love of God is a mandate for prophetic people. We accomplish this by daily evaluating our behaviors and attitudes toward God, ourselves, and others. These daily assessments must happen in the presence of the Lord because God is the best judge of our character and knows the journey and path we must take to become more like Christ. As we submit to the voice of God in the presence of the Lord, it will help us to be intentional about reflecting Christlike characteristics that can transform the world.

Here are some self-examination questions you can ask yourself at the end of each day during your time of worship or meditation on the Word of God. These questions can help you to assess your growth in God's love and identify areas where the Holy Spirit is leading you to love even more deeply.

- Where did I experience the love of God today?

- How did I express or demonstrate God's love today?

- Did I experience any offenses (feeling rejected, overlooked, undervalued, worried, or anxious) today that I need to pray and seek healing for and/or grant forgiveness?

Assess yourself in the presence of the Lord so that your time of self-evaluation doesn't become a self-loathing or self-praising event. God is a perfect judge of your heart. The Holy Spirit of God desires to go with you on this journey of growth. Be sure to submit and come into agreement with God's companionship on this journey to walk in love.

Spend some time in worship and then complete the daily love walk assessment to evaluate your day.

- Where did I experience the love of God today?

_____

_____

_____

_____

- How did I express or demonstrate God's love today?

_____

_____

_____

_____

- Did I experience any offenses (feeling rejected, overlooked, undervalued, worried, or anxious) today that I need to pray and seek healing for and/or grant forgiveness?

_____

_____

_____

Read 2 John 1:6.

How do we walk in the love of God?

_____

_____

_____

_____

_____

Worship, spending quiet time with God, and meditating on Scripture are some ways we can improve our love walk. What are some other things you can put into practice to improve your love walk?

_____

_____

_____

_____

Watch

This lesson's video teaching contains more about God's call to develop the nature and character of Christ as we prophesy the Lord's heart and mind to others. Watch the video segment titled "Ascend the Hill of the Lord."

Group Discussion

In a relationship with God we are invited to ascend the hill of the Lord and to go into God's secret place, where our hearts and motives are cleansed. On the ascent to the hill of the Lord, God brings conviction and definition to our character and calling. God desires to perfect our nature and our character so we become effective mouthpieces who can communicate the heart, Word, and love of God to others in a way that transforms the world. Therefore, it is so important that we allow the voice of God to help lead us into developing Christlike character. As you heard on the video, having godly character is significant because:

- Our character will determine the level of revelation and power the Lord will entrust to us.

- A lack of character development will result in blindness.

- Character development gives you the capacity to carry the authority of the kingdom.

This means that Christlike character gives you longevity in the face of life's trials, authority in the kingdom of God to be God's mouthpiece, and credibility before others that transforms the world.

The development of Christlike character gives our words power in the earth to transform lives. You are here and alive on the earth for this specific time because God has placed something within you that speaks to the condition of the world. Hidden within you are solutions and creative ideas that can make a world of difference to others. Many prophetic people do not get to fulfill this destiny because of opposition from the enemy. The first place the devil will attack as we journey to become more like Christ is the mouth. He will try to bring perversion and defamation to what we speak concerning ourselves and others. This will inherently pollute our prophetic flow and keep us from speaking the fullness of God's truth into the conditions of this world that we were born to solve.

Grab a partner, or as a group identify some of the sins of the mouth that can hinder the prophetic flow.

_____

_____

_____

_____

_____

As a group identify the root causes of the sins of the mouth you listed. How are we so often lured into committing these sins?

_____

_____

_____

_____

Think back to times when you committed sins of the mouth. Share with the group your experience. How do you think the sins of your mouth affected your witness of Christ's character to God and others?

_____

_____

_____

_____

As a group ask the Holy Spirit to identify some scriptures you all can meditate on as you grow into pure mouthpieces for God.

_____

_____

_____

_____

_____

Spend some time praying and declaring over your partner and those in the group what God desires for them to know about the power He has bestowed upon their words.

Action Plan

Ascending the hill of the Lord is a never-ending journey. As we yield to God's presence and His desire for our lives to reflect the nature and character of Christ, ascending the hill of the Lord becomes a lifestyle. It is a lifestyle of always seeking the voice of the Lord and walking in obedience to Him so others can experience God's transformation through you.

Commit today to pursuing the call to be God's prophetic mouthpiece with all diligence.

Meditate on 2 Peter 1:5–10. Ask God for a picture or a word that will help and encourage you to diligently pursue a deeper relationship with God through Christ

Jesus. Journal what God shares with you during your time of meditation.

_____

_____

_____

_____

_____

_____

_____

_____

_____

_____

_____

_____

_____

_____

_____

_____

_____

Notes

_____

_____

_____

_____

_____

_____

_____

_____

_____

_____

_____

_____

_____

_____

_____

_____

_____

_____

_____

_____

Notes

GO BUILD!

Through wisdom is a house built, and by understanding it is established.

—**PROVERBS 24:3**

THE MANDATE FOR those who can hear the voice of the Lord and who walk with a Christlike nature and character is to go forth and reproduce. The directive is to be a builder for the kingdom of God. This lesson will help you create blueprints for transforming the world according to God's prophetic pattern.

Review chapter 3 of *The Prophetic Advantage* book.

Read

In God's presence prophetic people receive several instructions from the Lord. You will receive directives for yourself concerning your life and your character, God will speak words of encouragement and instructions for others, and you will hear the mandate to build God's kingdom and God's bride, which is the church.

God's kingdom is always advancing through individuals like you who commit to building a legacy to the glory of God. Whenever God gives directives about our call, there will always be a component of that calling that has the power to transform the world. As we live out our calling to lead in the areas of business, religion, family, the arts and entertainment, government, education, media, or even to be a stay-at-home parent, God desires for us to be transformative leaders. We change the world when our leadership skills are partnered with a Christlike heart and our ability to hear God's voice. This positions us to be God's mouthpiece in our sphere of influence and glorify the name of Jesus in the process.

Our call to be transformative leaders also includes building Christ's bride, the church. You cannot call yourself a prophet or a prophetic person and only build in the marketplace while remaining outside the church. This is not the nature or the character of God. God is a God of order, and the Lord has set a pattern for us to build His kingdom. This pattern must include building the kingdom within your local church. The same skill sets and leadership capabilities God gives us to build His kingdom in the marketplace He also calls us to use to build within the local church.

The blueprint for building in the local church is found in Jesus's message to the seven churches in the Book of Revelation. Jesus set the prophetic pattern for building:

- Giving a commission to the senior leader

- Providing distinction to the church

- Revealing Christ's nature and character

- Bestowing the commendation

- Speaking to the areas in need of correction through the twofold challenge

- Granting a promise

Use the pages that follow to: (1) provide a brief description of each of these building blocks, (2) list how Scripture calls prophets and prophetic people to use the building blocks to build up the body of Christ, and (3) write how, through your ideas or skill sets, you can use the building blocks to build in your local church. Review pages 38–42 of *The Prophetic Advantage* for more information about the prophetic pattern.

Giving a commission to the senior leader

- Definition

_____

_____

_____

_____

_____

- How prophetic people are called to use this
  building block to build God's kingdom

_____

_____

_____

_____

_____

- How God is calling me to use this building
  block to build His kingdom

_____

_____

_____

_____

_____

Providing distinction to the church

- Definition

_____

_____

_____

_____

_____

- How prophetic people are called to use this building block to build God's kingdom

_____

_____

_____

_____

- How God is calling me to use this building block to build His kingdom

_____

_____

_____

_____

Revealing Christ's nature and character

- Definition

_____

_____

_____

_____

_____

- How prophetic people are called to use this building block to build God's kingdom

_____

_____

_____

_____

- How God is calling me to use this building block to build His kingdom

_____

_____

_____

_____

Bestowing the commendation

- Definition

_____

_____

_____

_____

_____

- How prophetic people are called to use this building block to build God's kingdom

_____

_____

_____

_____

- How God is calling me to use this building block to build His kingdom

_____

_____

_____

_____

Speaking to the areas in need of correction through the twofold challenge

- Definition

_____

_____

_____

_____

_____

- How prophetic people are called to use this building block to build God's kingdom

_____

_____

_____

_____

- How God is calling me to use this building block to build His kingdom

_____

_____

_____

_____

_____

Granting a promise

- Definition

_____

_____

_____

_____

_____

- How prophetic people are called to use this
  building block to build God's kingdom

_____

_____

_____

_____

_____

- How God is calling me to use this building
  block to build His kingdom

_____

_____

_____

_____

_____

Use the following section to provide a brief description of what these different building blocks mean for a local church. Then create a list of how prophets and prophetic people are called to build up the body of Christ using this prophetic building block. Once you have defined the step in the prophetic pattern and the directive God gave in Scripture on how to accomplish that step, write ideas or skill sets you have that can be used in your local church to build using that particular building block. Review pages 38–42 in *The Prophetic Advantage* for more information about the prophetic pattern.

Personal Discovery

Now that you know the definitions of the various steps in the prophetic pattern, the directives God has given in Scripture on how to accomplish these steps, and the skill sets and ideas you have to accomplish these tasks, it's time for you to build. This is where having a prophetic advantage will be helpful because you can pray and ask God to show you exactly where He is leading you to build His church in this season of your life. Even though you may have ideas and abilities to build according to several building blocks in the prophetic pattern, that does not mean God is calling you to build in every part of the church all at once. It is important to pray and ask God for revelation on the areas in which He is guiding you to build.

Pray and ask God to show you how He is calling you to build in the local church in this season. Circle that area in the prophetic pattern exercise chart. Ask God for the best strategy you can use within your local church to build up His church in this particular area. Ask God for the individuals you can connect with to accomplish what He has called you to do. Ask Him what training or mentors you need to build to His glory in this area of your local church. Ask God whom you can mentor as you build in this area. Document your answers below.

1. The best strategy I can use within my local church to build according to the prophetic pattern is:

_____

_____

_____

_____

2. The individuals I can connect with to accomplish what God has called me to build in my local church are:

_____

_____

_____

_____

_____

3. The training or mentors I need to build to God's glory in this area of my local church are:

_____

_____

_____

_____

_____

4. God is calling me to mentor the following individuals as I build within the local church:

_____

_____

_____

_____

_____

Reflect

Prophets and prophetic people do not just come out of a cave and prophesy. We also have the responsibility to equip the church. We are foundation layers and builders. Prophets and prophetic people are called to lay the foundation by equipping and perfecting the church. True prophets and prophetic people build by teaching, assisting, and arming the individuals in their local church with the strategies and skills they need to accomplish the work of ministry both in the church and in the world. We accomplish this by teaching others how to have "God consciousness" and how to release God's consciousness in the earth. When we who can hear the voice of God for ourselves and others build in this manner, it causes the prophetic gift to become a blessing to the body of Christ and to the world. We become a blessing to our local church and glorify God as we transform the world.

It is also important to remember that building in the local church will not always be perfect. As we set our hearts to assist in training and equipping the members of the church, and sending believers to make disciples of nations, challenges may arise. Second Corinthians 2:11 reminds us not to be ignorant of Satan's schemes against us. So we must acknowledge that on our journey of becoming God's mouthpiece that will transform the world, there will be challenges and hardship. Unfortunately, this is not a new phenomenon; since its formation the local church has faced opposition. Revelation 2:1–3:22 documents challenges that oftentimes plague the local church.

Make a list of the challenges the seven churches faced according to Revelation 2:1–3:22.

_____

_____

_____

_____

_____

_____

_____

_____

_____

_____

_____

_____

_____

Pray and ask God to help you see the challenges in
your local church. Then ask how the Lord desires to
use you to be a solution to these challenges. Journal
what God reveals to you in the space provided.

_____

_____

_____

_____

_____

_____

_____

_____

_____

_____

_____

_____

Remember, our prophetic advantage makes us a blessing to everyone we meet. Our ability to prophetically discern the challenges of our local church or within someone's life is only the first of many steps God will hold us accountable to accomplish. Once we determine the challenges, we must ask God for the solution. God may call us to share the solution or to become the solution; either way, we must commit to walk in obedience.

Watch

In this last video teaching we'll hear some additional tips and advice on building in the local church to the glory of God. Watch the video segment titled "Go Build."

Group Discussion

The video teaching reminds us that those who can hear the voice of God for themselves and others are called to build the church. Prophets and prophetic people are tasked to lay the foundations within the church and strengthen the mission and ministry of the local church. In the marketplace as well as within the local church, building is a team sport. Prophets and prophetic people must work together with the Holy Spirit, other prophetic individuals, pastors, apostles, teachers, evangelists, and all members of the church and community to build the kingdom of God.

Grab a partner and share some of the plans God has given you for building in your local church. Have your partner share the ways God is calling him or her to build in the local church. Identify areas of similarity

and possible partnerships where you and your partner
can work together to build the kingdom of God. Be
sure to pray and ask God for guidance and wisdom.
Journal any insights, plans, strategies, or details you
receive during your time of prayer.

_____

_____

_____

_____

_____

Change partners and share the challenges God
revealed to you concerning your local church. Ask
your partner to share what God revealed concerning
the challenges within his or her local church. Spend
some time praying for each other and for the solutions
God has revealed. Journal any prophetic insight you
receive during your prayer time with your partner.

_____

_____

_____

_____

_____

_____

Action Plan

Use the next few months to implement the strategies, blueprints, and solutions God has given you to build up the local church.

Schedule some time with the mentor you identified in prayer. Share with that person the strategy, training, and the individual whom God has called you to mentor. Create an accountability process with your mentor, empowering that person to encourage and evaluate you as you build within the local church.

Notes

Notes

Notes

Notes

_____

_____

_____

_____

_____

_____

_____

_____

_____

_____

_____

_____

_____

_____

_____

_____

_____

_____

_____

_____

FINAL NOTES

CONGRATULATIONS ON COMPLETING *The Prophetic Advantage Study Guide*. The completion of this workbook marks the beginning of your never-ending journey to becoming a mouthpiece for God who transforms the world. Your commitment to hearing the voice of God, ascending the hill of the Lord to become more like Christ, and building up the local church must be continual.

On this journey I encourage you to make your relationship with God through Jesus Christ your primary pursuit. When the presence of the Lord becomes our primary pursuit, the Holy Spirit transforms us in such a way that we become change agents in the world. So don't let being a prophet, a prophetic person, or a mouthpiece be your primary pursuit. Nor should you let transforming the world be your primary pursuit. God loves you. His primary concern is not your ministry; it is you as an individual. Therefore, as you embark on this new commitment to walk in the fullness of your prophetic advantage, live your life in such a way that you cultivate a heart that seeks relationship with God above all else.

ABOUT THE AUTHOR

MICHELLE MCCLAIN-WALTERS HAS traveled to more than fifty nations and has conducted prophetic schools that have activated thousands in the art of hearing God's voice. The author of *The Deborah Anointing*, *The Esther Anointing*, *The Anna Anointing*, and *The Prophetic Advantage*, Michelle currently serves as director of prayer ministry at Crusaders Church, under the leadership of Apostle John Eckhardt. She is an international and national conference speaker. She is also an apostolic team leader for The Impact Network. Michelle resides in Chicago with her husband, Pastor Floyd A. Walters Jr.

CONNECT WITH US!

CHARISMA HOUSE

(Spiritual Growth)

f Facebook.com/CharismaHouse

🐦 @CharismaHouse

📷 Instagram.com/CharismaHouse

SILOAM

(Health)

📌 Pinterest.com/CharismaHouse

MEV MODERN ENGLISH VERSION

(Bible)

www.mevbible.com